GOODWIN SEMAKEN

Kaltag

SPIRIT MOUNTAIN PRESS

GOODWIN SEMAKEN

Kaltag

ISBN: 0-910871-08-6

Interviewing and Editing:
Yvonne Yarber and Curt Madison

Photography:
Curt Madison (unless otherwise noted)

Material collected September 1979, April 1982 in Kaltag, Alaska.

Manuscript approved by Goodwin Semaken April 1983.

SPIRIT MOUNTAIN PRESS
P.O. BOX 1214 FAIRBANKS, ALASKA 99707

Produced and Funded by:
Yukon-Koyukuk School District of Alaska

Regional School Board:
Donald V. Honea - Chairman
Eddie Bergman - Vice Chairman
Luke Titus - Secretary
Pat Madros - Treasurer
Fred Lee Bifelt

Superintendent: Joe Cooper
Assistant Superintendent: Fred Lau
Project Coordinator: Don Kratzer

Supplemental funding:
Johnson O'Malley Grant - EOOC14202516

**Library of Congress
Cataloging in Publication Data**

Madison, Curt
Yarber, Yvonne
    Semaken, Goodwin - Kaltag. A Biography
    YKSD Biography Series
    ISBN 0-910871-08-6

1. Semaken, Goodwin 2. Koyukon-Athabaskan
3. Alaska Biography

Frontispiece:

L-R, Front: 1. ?, Jeanine, Christina Semaken, Craig Semaken, Daryl, 2 children, Julie, Diane, Goodwin Sr., Back row: Margaret Commack, Jackie, Goodwin Jr., Betty with son Jeramie, Kenny, Chris.

A Note From a Linguist

As you read through this autobiography you will notice a style and a diction you may not have seen before in print. This is because it is an oral storytelling style. This autobiography has been compiled from many hours of taped interviews. As you read you should listen for the sound of the spoken voice. While it has not been possible to show all the rhythms and nuances of the speaker's voice, much of the original style has been kept. If posssible you should read aloud and use your knowledge of the way the old people speak to recapture the style of the original.

This autobiography has been written in the original style for three reasons. First, the original style is a kind of dramatic poetry that depends on pacing, succinctness, and semantic indirectness for its narrative impact. The original diction is part and parcel of its message and the editors have kept that diction out of a deep respect for the person represented in this autobiography.

The second reason for keeping the original diction is that it gives a good example of some of the varied richness of the English language. English as it is spoken in many parts of the world and by many different people varies in style and the editors feel that it is important for you as a reader to know, understand and respect the wide resources of this variation in English.

The third reason for writing in the original style is that this style will be familiar to many of you who will read this book. The editors hope that you will enjoy reading something in a style that you may never have seen written before even though you have heard it spoken many times.

Ron Scollon
Alaska Native Language Center
University of Alaska
Fairbanks
1979

Acknowledgements

As with other books in this series, many people have helped. Bob Maguire donated the original idea and has since escaped to the Kobuk. Ron Scollon and family continue linguistics/computer work in Haines. Eliza Jones, Alaska Native Language Center-University of Alaska, has donated translation and correct orthography of Koyukon words. In Kaltag, Glenn, Hazel, Arlo, Tassie, and Drew generously provided a place to stay. Nathan Kyle, principal of Kaltag School, did much more than necessary to facilitate our time with Goodwin. John Lyle, photographer and teacher, allowed us to use one of his slides. Carmen and Kevin Le Fevour helped with captions. Liza Vernet and Janis Carney of Manley Hot Springs donate their time as proofreaders. Joe Cooper, Fred Lau, and Mavis Brown of the Yukon-Koyukuk School District Central Office keep the ball rolling. Members of the Regional School Board remain committed to the local curriculum through this and other projects. The staff of Spirit Mountain Press brought this book into final print: Larry Laraby owner and manager, Doug Miller graphic artist and Eva Bee the indispensable typesetter.

Thank you.

Foreword

This book is the sixteenth produced by the Yukon-Koyukuk School District in a series meant to provide cultural understanding of our own area and relevant role models for students. Too often Interior Alaska is ignored in books or mentioned only in conjunction with its mineral resources such as the gold rush or oil pipeline. We are gauged by what we are worth to Outside people. People living in the Interior certainly have been affected by those things but also by missionaries, wage labor, fur prices, celebrations, spring hunts, schools, technology, potlatches, and much more. For residents, Interior Alaska is all of those things people do together, whether in the woods, on the river, in the village or on Two Street. It's a rich and varied culture often glossed over in favor of things more easily written and understood.

This project was begun in 1977 by Bob Maguire. Representatives of Indian Education Parent Committees from each of Yukon-Koyukuk School District's eleven villages met in Fairbanks February of 1978 to choose two people from each village to write about. A variety of selection means were used—from school committees to village council elections. Despite the fact that most of the representatives were women, few women were chosen for the books. As the years passed, more women were added to give a more complete accounting of recent cultural changes.

It is our goal to provide a vehicle for people who live around us so they can describe the events of their lives in their own words. To be singled out as an individual as we have done in this series has not always been comfortable for the biographees, particularly for those who carry the strong Koyukon value of being humble. Talking about oneself has been a conflict overridden by the desire and overwhelming need to give young people some understanding of their own history in a form they have become accustomed to. A growing number of elders who can't read or write themselves think young people won't believe anything unless it's written in a book. This project attempts to give oral knowledge equal time in the schools.

As materials of this kind become more common, methods of gathering and presenting oral history get better. The most important ingredient is trust. After many hours of interview, people often relax to the point of saying some personal things they prefer left unpublished. After editing the tape transcripts we bring the rough draft manuscript back to the biographees to let them add or delete things before it becomes public. Too often those of us living in rural Alaska have been researched *on* or written *about* for an audience far away. This series is meant to bring information full round--from us back to us for our own uses.

Too many people in the Interior have felt ripped-off by journalists and bureaucrats. Hundreds pass through every year, all wanting information and many never to return. Occasionally their finished work may find its way back to the source only to flare emotions when people feel misrepresented. Perhaps a tight deadline or the lack of travel money may be the excuse for not returning for verification or approval. That is no consolation for people who opened up and shared something of themselves and are left feeling betrayed. We work closely with the biographees to check facts and intentions. The books need to be intimate and daring but the last thing we want to do is make someone's life more difficult. We need to share information in a wholesome way. After all, we're all in this together.

Comments about the biographies, their use, corrections, questions, or anything else is welcome.

Curt Madison
Yvonne Yarber
December 10, 1982
Manley Hot Springs
Alaska 99756

Table Of Contents

Introduction

Goodwin Semaken lives in Kaltag, an Athabaskan village of under 300 people. It is on the Yukon River side of a portage trail to Unalakleet on the Bering Sea coast. His mother was Inupiat and his father Koyukon. He has relatives in two cultures. Goodwin was born the year Kaltag moved to its present site, he and the village are the same age. His parents lived off the land before people stayed year-round in one place. His children are at home in cities.

Goodwin is a man of smiling wisdom able to do what he advocates. His hunting skill, business sense, creativity and love for children are well demonstrated to everyone in Kaltag. His life bridges Eskimo, Indian, and White cultures and he has learned the languages of each one. We would do well to listen to him.

Making camp coffee while enjoying spring break-up on the banks of the Yukon River at Kaltag, May 1982. L-R: Goodwin Semaken Sr., Junior Solomon, Sebastian McGinty Sr., Simon Stanley.

Glossary

ASHA - Alaska State Housing Authority

AVEC - Alaska Village Electrical Cooperative

gee-pole - a pole attached to the front of a dogsled and held by a person on skiis to keep the sled on a narrow trail while it is pulled by dogs.

Kaiyuh - or *Kkaayah* refers to the flats between the Kaiyuh Mountains and Yukon River, an area which has long been used for hunting and trapping.

kicker - outboard motor for boats

PHS - Public Health Service

sun-dry fish - salmon cut and preserved by drying in the sun rather than in a smokehouse.

Local Area

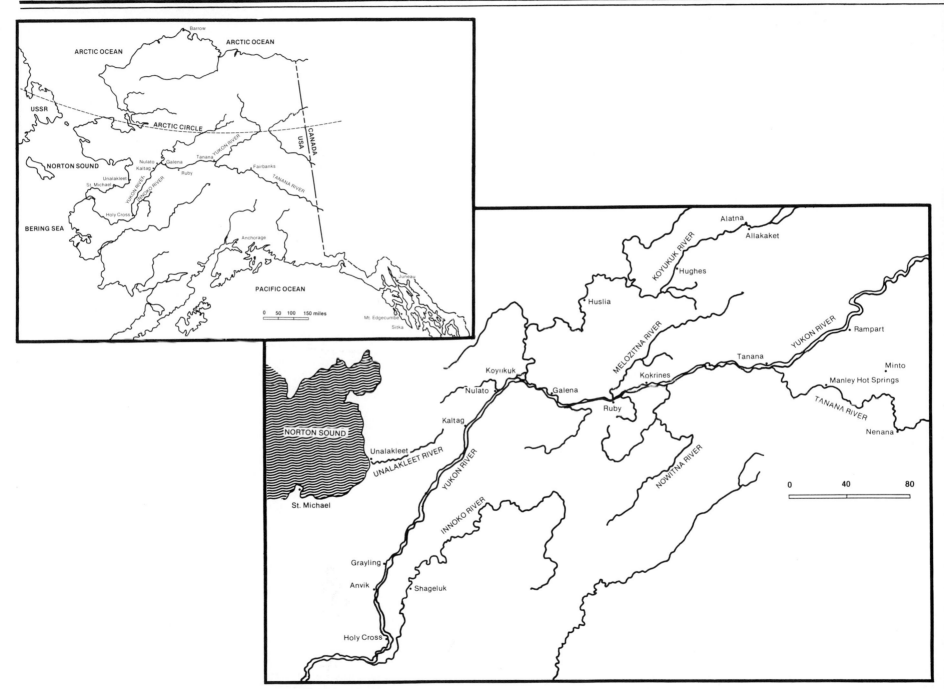

Arlo Olsen in the one-dog race at the Kaltag Spring Carnival April 1983.

Goodwin carrying a covered dish to the community hall during the Kaltag Stickdance April 1983.

Kaltag on the Yukon River, May 1982.

Kaltag, May 1982.

Front Street in Kaltag. Taken from the Yukon River, September 1979.

13

Chapter One: Young Kid

Father

My father was from downriver. He said before my time there were lots of caribou around there. The Native name is *Sislaakkaakk'at*, like you're saying bear, so in English they call it Bear Creek. There was no village, just maybe a couple families stayed there. Old-timers never looked for a village like Kaltag to live in. There were no jobs. Only income in Kaltag then would be the postmaster and teacher. Postmaster owned the store and only one single teacher. That would be the only income. So these people didn't have a village down at Bear Creek. They just stop there because it was a good area for fish or caribou.

No tents then, either, or log cabins. They used to have real mud houses. I think that was the best kind of warm house there was. Warmer than the log cabins we have now. They call them *naahalooyah*. About average size was 10' by 10'. They had a fire right in the middle. No stove just a hole in the roof. All the smoke would draw up there. I was never in one, but when I was 15 or 16 I saw some that were already caving in. That's the kind our parents were living in.

Before Kaltag moved up from the old town a few miles below here my dad got pretty sick. He couldn't do nothing for his family. I wasn't born yet. My brother-in-law who is married to my cousin brought the family up to Nulato to the Mission. Sisters, brothers and a priest in Nulato. And they had a clinic. That's the closest place they could go by dog team so my brother-in-law brought my dad and my mother and the family up. They stayed by the mission for several years. All the time after that he had to go to church.

Even if he had to crawl he wouldn't miss Easter Mass.

Christmas was the same way. All those Catholic holidays he wouldn't go out and split wood. But he didn't like Independence Day, Fourth of July or St. Patrick's Day. He said because that's just a time for people to be happy. To make one another happy and drink. Well, my dad was quite a drinker, too, but he was like me. He think about his family more than drink. He never refused a drink from anybody. But he wouldn't overdo himself with the drink. When we used to go out trapping he used to have a bottle of whiskey with him all the time. Every night after getting through work, he used to take one drink and then go to bed.

He had a fish trap sixteen miles down here on the island. He used to catch trout, grayling, lush, sheefish, and whitefish. All different kinds of fish in that trap. It was really good, but I never learned how to put one in. Wintertime under the ice, I mean. Eddie Hildebrand in Nulato has one.

Photo by Jetté, circa 1910. Oregon Province Jesuit Archives

L-R: George Semaken, Manook, Hooligan, Timothy Number Two

My dad made his trap all out of spruce and willows. He used to say anytime you put iron in the water, the fish don't like it. He was quite a bit superstitious about fishing, because fish in the water, like bears hibernating, don't make tracks. When he brought up the first fish he wouldn't pass it around until the next day. It had to stay overnight in the cache first. Later when you bring fish up from the trap, if somebody buy it before you bring it inside your house or cache, that's fine. But the rest, if you keep it or put it away, it has to be there overnight.

He was the same way about black bear. He said there's some girls don't eat black bear because they could give you bad luck. You wouldn't find a bear again easy. It's hard to catch black bear anyway in the fall because there's no snow. They hibernate early in the fall and that's all. You walk around just like you lost something in the woods looking for bear den. Pretty soon you don't even catch anything. You don't even see a sign of it. You can spend days and days out hunting, looking around for black bear in the dens and you'll never catch it. So he was right.

Sometimes he did get a black bear in the fall. The fat was about couple inches thick on the back. We always put that away for special time like New Year's canvas toss. People come around shaking a canvas in front of your door and you throw in some food. Then they take it all to the community center and potlatch it out to people. They cut the bear fat into strips because it was very valuable. That's just about the richest food there was for falltime.

Mother

My mother was from out Unalakleet way. They call it Reindeer Station in English but in Native it is *K'inaakkoy Nuggut*. My mother was raised there so she is part Eskimo. The rest is Indian. I don't know her parents' names. She didn't know herself. She said she was pretty small when her father died, but big when her mother died.

There was a trail through *K'inaakkoy Nuggut* between Kaltag and Unalakleet. The only place there was store before the one here came up was in St. Michael and Unalakleet. N.C. Co. had big outfits in those places. Lot of people from the Yukon used to go over there to get groceries. Five dogs was the most people had. Some just with three or four and some pulling their toboggan on foot.

Kaltag is not a really old village. It's people from all the surrounding areas. Some came from Innoko River. Some came from seventy miles down the Yukon at *Sislaakkaakk'at* and from down further. Some came from nearby and some from *K'inaakkoy Nuggut*. Slim Rubin, John Chiroskey and Old Man Stanley all came from Reindeer Station.

When I was about 8 or 9 they used to bring a herd of reindeer over. Practically all the Unalakleet people had a herd of their own. Hardly any moose or caribou so when the trader here wanted some reindeer they just herded them over. They camped about a mile back from town. They corralled them, kill them off, and butcher them right there. I've seen it. They sell the meat to the store or traders in Nulato. Then they would give us all the extras like the head or hoofs or skin. Whatever they can't sell they give to the Natives.

Born

I was born here at Kaltag December 21, 1920. That was about the year people moved the village up from the Old Village. A trader came and built a store here so people wanted to be closer to it. Jim Addison was the first store owner. Adolf Miller was the next one. He was married to Edgar Kalland's mother's sister. Along with the store Adolf had a pool table. After he died people say his spirit still rolled the balls around with no one else there. He is buried on the bank by the old church.

Then another guy came and bought the store. He was a mail carrier. They used to have a mail run on the Yukon by dog team. And the same time the main line for mail service to Anchorage and Fairbanks was through the portage here to Unalakleet. No airplanes in those days. During the summer they packed the mail on foot. Each man could carry only seventy-five pounds. Over to Unalakleet there are six creeks about as big as the Kaltag River, some much bigger. They had bridges across all of them for summer packing, spring when there's hardly any snow left on the ground, and fall before the ice freezes good. Since they're used mostly for walking I call them foot-bridges.

Ninety miles from here to Unalakleet and the trail was good. Not growed in like now. They had mail cabins at 22 Mile, forty miles out, what they used to call 10 Mile, one at Old Woman, fifty miles out and one more at Whaleback named after a crippled man, twenty-three miles out of Unalakleet. At all those cabins they had a telephone. No satellite phone like we have now. It was a wire running all the way from St. Michael to Tanana and beyond.

John Sommers, a White guy, had the mail contract here. His house was just about where my place is now. He used to hire some Natives to pack mail for him. And those days there used to be a lot of mail. Summertime you carry only first class mail, but just about the end of the season after they buy fur in April you used to carry hundreds of pounds of mail by dogteam.

I was a little boy when I used to go with my dad. He carried mail from Nulato to 40 Mile out here. His dogs were too rough to handle alone in the beginning of the season, falltime, so he used to take me out of school to hold the brake for him. He had to hold the gee-pole at the bow of the sleigh and stand on skis. That's the only way he could keep the sleigh on the trail because the load was so heavy. We'd have eight or nine hundred pounds of mail on every trip. He couldn't handle that much load from the handlebar. And whenever there were any rabbits or ptarmigans on the road, he'd have a tough time holding the dogs back.

One trip I'll never forget. When my oldest sister got married to Clement Esmailka I went to live with them in the fall. We stayed out in Kaiyuh. Then my dad sent word up that he needed me to come back to hold the brake for him on his mail team. The dogs were too rough to hold especially if there was a light load coming back. We took a heavy load out then we turned around at 10 Mile, that's forty miles from here. And only had ten pounds of mail to bring back in. That's not much load for thirteen dogs. Especially since we had one dog that liked to bark and jolly up the dogs. He'd get them to run and gallop.

That morning my brother left ahead of us with his team. He was trapping out that way. Boy, those dogs could smell the fresh trail of his team ahead.

They really got going. My dad had a four inch by eight inch brake and I stood on that brake almost the whole way. Well, that's why I went with him. It's not level, either, some places are pretty steep.

Ten miles out from here we stopped at a creek. The creek was frozen over so we weren't going to use the bridge but the bank was eight foot and steep. He told me to hold the brake so he can get off the gee-pole and put the skis in the sled. He wanted to ride the runners and let me carry the skis across the creek. I got off the sled. Just as he got on the handlebar the dogs started barking. They took off. He held the brake all the way down into the creek, up the bank, and into the woods. By the time I got up the bank he was gone. I couldn't see him anymore. Only fresh snow where he was holding the brake into the trail. I stop and listen. I could hear him hollering quite a ways up ahead. I was just only a little boy. I got scared and started crying, but I never stopped running.

I ran about a mile and came out in an open flat. That flat was about a mile long but I still couldn't see him. Running, running. I could see places where he caught onto old stumps with the snubbing line. Old stumps where guys cut wood long time ago by the trail. Too old I guess. He pulled them right out. I keep running and keep holding onto those skis. Four miles I chase after him.

Finally at 6 Mile I found him. He rammed his sleigh down in the creek into the willows. He was standing in front of the leader with his ax trying to keep those dogs quiet. Threaten them. Try to scare them and keep them from jerking. "Okay, my son," he said, "get in the sleigh. We're going to make those dogs *go* next six miles!"

I sat in the sleigh while he broke off some little willows to scare the dogs. He make those dogs gallop all the way in for six miles. He was mad. "Gee, those dogs are pretty rough," he said. That was the first time I was alone in the woods.

The next day he went to Nulato and came back with three or four hundred pounds. He said, "You don't have to come with me son." So I went back to school. That's why I didn't have much schooling. I was the only other boy left at home. I had six brothers but they were all out trapping. I had to go with my dad when he needed me. Out of nine months of school I only went about four months. And I went only as far as fourth grade.

In those days you could go up to sixth grade, then you were done with school. There was not a high school that you could go to. Mt. Edgecumbe school wasn't open yet. Later on it started to get a little bit better. After I quit school. Well, after you're 16 then you're done with school, too.

Sometimes here there would be only four students from September on. All the parents would go out in September and stay out till December. Come back. Then January we're all out in our camps again. In those days you had to stay out and live off the country. There was no mail plane. No fresh food like eggs we're getting right now. Only time we get our fresh food is in the beginning of the spring in June and the last boat in September. Twice a year, that's all we used to get some eggs or some fresh food. All the rest of the time we just had to live off the land. When we want to get something fresh then we had to go out and kill it.

My family had five boys and three girls when I was growing up. We all stayed in one building. I remember Dad used to get fifty pounds of flour pretty near about twice a week. That's the sweetest thing we could get. And my brother used to bake bread. Eight loaves and that bread would only last one day. Next day he'd have to bake some more.

My parents were really busy. My mother was out every day trying to catch something for us. Out snaring rabbits, or ptarmigans or go to fishnet. If Dad was out trapping he

Photo by Jetté, Oregon Province Jesuit Archives

Goodwin's parents. L-R: Lizzy, Wilfred, Tassie and George Semaken in Kaltag, circa 1910.

might be on the trapline for thirty days. During that time we had no extra dogs so we had to haul wood out by our neck or pack it out. At least wood was close at that time. Right now you have to go quite a ways back to get wood because it's all chopped out. Things were way different in those days.

My parents didn't know much English. My mother didn't speak English at all. They didn't see many White people around here. In fact, we used to be scared of White people when we were kids. If some White guy come down, some miner come down in a boat, we'd be scared of him. We wouldn't even talk with him. Maybe we'd be about thirty or forty feet away from him watching. Now these days, some stranger comes into town, you see a little boy or little girl go up and start talking with him. "Where you come from? What you're doing?" And all those questions. My days we never used to do that because there was only one White man here, the guy that's buried on the bank, Adolf Miller. Plus the school teacher would come in the falltime.

After the school teacher came there used to be a curfew. They ring the bell every night and you got to go in. If they catch you out your parents have a fine, like fifty cents or twenty-five cents. They thought it was good for us for the beginning of our schooling. My parents didn't really go for it. They didn't want me to learn. They didn't want me to go to school. They said that was just wasting time. They wanted me to learn out in the woods. I was the youngest boy in the family and my dad was trying to spoil me I guess. Tried to make a pet out of me. But my brothers Burke and Benjamin went to school at Holy Cross. My oldest brother stayed there nine full years. Never came home on vacation. Nine full years at the mission.

Chapter Two: Do It For Myself

Lost

There were quite a few times after my dad quit carrying mail I used to go out trapping with him. He never run but he was a fast walker. Most of the time I had to run to keep with him. I was 10 or 12 at that time and I had to keep up running. When you're a kid, you have a lot of energy and you never feel it if you get tired or not. If you take two or three minutes rest then you are ready to go again. So that's the way it was. He used to get away from me, but I could catch him up running. Then that way I got a little bit braver. Staying in the woods behind him. That way I got used to be alone. Pretty soon then I started to go trapping alone. The longer I trapped the better I like it. I go a long ways in the woods and sometimes don't even notice that the darkness is already coming in on me. By the time I get back to camp it's pretty dark. November days are short. By eight or nine o'clock I walked four or five hours in the dark. It doesn't bother me. Sometimes I start out in the dark in the morning. Sometimes I wait for the daylight and sometimes I just go whenever I want.

I had a flashlight but batteries were very valuable. You only used the light to check traps then put it away again to save the batteries. Especially if you were out for two or three months. After I got married I never stayed out that long because I had to make sure my family had wood and enough food. Longest I'd be out would be couple weeks then back in town again. Stay in town for another week to haul in wood and water and get ready to go out again.

Walking is what I used to enjoy the most. Walking, you take in everything and enjoy the scenery. In good weather I spot some trees or lakes or hills to go by because it's easy to get lost. If you're in thick woods with no openings you'll always get lost. I know. I do all the time. Therefore, if I'm out in the woods and I don't know where I'm at, I kind of spot from one tree to another to see if I made a circle. I always get lost in the woods. My father used to tell me the best thing to do if you're getting lost is to turn around and follow your tracks. I never did that. I always think I could make it and it seems like I get worse everytime I try. I go in a circle and then pretty soon cross my track and I don't know where I'm at. Storm is worse yet.

One December, Simon Stanley and me were trapping up here about fifteen miles inland. That time we went together on the trail. It was close to Christmastime. I asked him to make a shortcut. We came out in a lake and I never seen that lake before. And open place past there. I asked him where we were and he said he don't know, too. So we crossed that lake and went in the woods on the other side. We were going according to the wind. Pretty soon we come back in that lake again. I don't know how we turned around. I told him, "Gee, we're lost. I don't know where we're going now. Let's go kind of face that wind and then maybe one of us could recognize our trapline."

We started out again the same way. We walk back in the woods and every once in awhile we stopped and look at the trees to see which way the wind is blowing. According to that we walked. We keep on walking. Pretty soon we hit our trapline and then we know where we're at. We could tell by the wind how to go. Wintertime we usually get a north wind. Summer is the south wind. If you see a star or the moon or the sun, it does the same thing to spot your way.

I have heard from different people about keeping my way. They say whenever you go always spot the way. Look at the ground or the trees or which way the wind has been blowing. Or like in falltime it rains and the trees get iced up. Usually the ice is on the north side. If you watch all those things you can get lost and still survive all right. Just know what you're

23

doing and don't get excited.

That's the reason I'd like to have a men's club like the women's club. Get together and have a meeting. I know a lot of the young guys would get lost in the woods and not know what to do. They wouldn't know how to survive because they never hear anybody talk to them about how to survive. As long as you have an ax and matches you could survive pretty easy. But they usually just want to keep going and going until they get real tired. It happened like that here a couple years ago with Raymond Nickoli, Jr.

He went across in the flats out hunting and got lost. A good thing about people here is if somebody is lost they all just gather up and start in hunting for them. Searching for the guy. Bad weather you can get lost easy and it's hard to track you. Wind blowing and snow coming into the tracks.

I wasn't here that time, but they said those guys were out there a whole night and whole day looking for him. Couldn't find him. Finally they find him not far away from here already passed out. Lucky it was warm. He was so tired. He just keep on walking and walking and walking. Never think about making fire. Walking till he drop.

Running

When I was growing up my dad told me he used to get out of bed in the morning and run around in the snow. "That's the only way you're going to be any good," he said. In the falltime before there's a little snow on the ground I'd get up and run out. Cut some wood, bring it and make a camp fire. He always said that's the best exercise you got. Before you take anything, even water or tea or a piece of bread. You'd be a good runner. Better if you run a mile or so every morning. You got to depend on that if you ever go after anything like bear or moose.

Caribou is easy he'd say. The bunch just go so far then stop and wait for you. You still got to be a fast runner because they're fast. But moose is

Starting line at the Kaltag Carnival Snowshoe race, April 1983. L-R: Ralph Silas, Ronnie Pitka, Darrell Semaken, Billy Demoski, Hazel Olson.

worse. He hear you once or he smell you once, that's it. He wouldn't wait for you. That's where you're going to have a tough time. That's when you need your power to catch that animal. If you don't know how to hunt it, you'll never get a moose.

So I used to run everyday. I used to run from here down to 22 Mile. Never stop running on snowshoes. All the way down and back. I told my kids that. What we used to do when we were that age. And I was watching them playing basketball back here. Kids last only about ten minutes then they'd be puffing. Out of wind. "Why you're like that" I said. "You're supposed to be better than that. It's because you only take exercise when you have to. You got to keep it up every day in order to be in good shape. I know it," I tell them. "I done it for myself."

Kids right now wouldn't believe me. If it's not written down in a book they wouldn't believe you. How hard we used to work to catch our moose. I'll talk more about that later.

When you run everyday you can go long ways before you get tired. There is one time, though, I drop. I drop right there at the foot of the hill over the bank from my house. I blame myself for it. Me and my brother Benjamin was out trapping. We came up twenty or thirty miles to our camp, 22 Mile. He had six good dogs, but my brothers never used to give me a ride. As long as I was young they wouldn't give me a ride with their dogs. I ran behind them or ahead of them.

We got to 22 Mile about three o'clock in the afternoon. We checked our beaver traps. Benjamin said he's going to stay overnight but that seems too long for me. Another day would be too long for me. I told him I was going on to Kaltag. I was single and I was thinking about my girlfriend up here. I told him I want to go to Kaltag so I just put on my snowshoes and nothing — no ax, no gun, not even a bite to eat. I just took off there. Start in running.

Run part of the way and I start to get

hungry. About eight miles below here I got thirsty. I want a drink of water. Nothing to drink water in so I break some ice, rough ice that was sticking out of the snow. I break it off and chew it. Keep on walking and running part of the time. Pretty soon it start to get dark on me. Seems like I was trying to go fast.

When I got to the bank down here, I couldn't come up the bank. I was that tired. I couldn't come up the hill I was so hungry. Mostly hungry and wanted a drink. I think about all the good things that I wanted to eat and drink. Then I lay down there and I fall asleep.

That's the worst thing you can do when you panic is to lay down. If you just sit up you're all right. I lay down on the snow and went to sleep for about ten minutes. Then I woke up and started to go up the bank. I was just staggering going up. Barely make it to the house over there. Then I drank water and passed out. I must have run forty or fifty miles that day. My brother used to get up early on the trapline. We had plenty of time. I walked, I don't run. But myself I never learned my lesson. Everytime I go somewhere, like if I'm going to Nulato I do the same thing. I run.

Start To Have Dogs

I never had dogs till after I got married. Before that people say, "He's a young guy. He could run." They wouldn't put me on the sleigh. My old man would let me run ahead of dogs if there was no trail. Or if the dogs are going fast, we run behind. In those days no young guys ride on the sleigh. They believe in that. My brothers were the same way. So I listen to different people on experience with dogs. How to take care of dogs and what are good dogs. I was thinking to myself I'm going to have good dogs when I grow up. You know, if I start to have my own team, my own family, I'm going to have good dogs.

After I got married, I bought one dog with three in a litter. I already had one dog my brother was using and it had three, too. So I had six pups and two older dogs. We had a camp one mile up here and a fish wheel there. Every morning I get the best fish out and cook it for the dogs. Then I have my breakfast while it cools down. I feed it to my six pups. Dinnertime same way. If there was some left over from morning I throw it out and cook fresh pot for them. In the evening same thing again. I just continue that all summer.

The pups were so small, but I start in running with them. I turned their mother loose and run for a mile with them every morning. Sometimes they'd be quite a ways behind me. Pretty soon, about a month's time, those little pups keep up with me. A month later I couldn't get away from those dogs. They were behind me or ahead of me all the time. They were good because I gave them exercise the same time I was giving myself exercise, too.

That fall we went out to our camp at 22 Mile. I had one little girl already at that time. I fished for those pups down there, too. Three months old and I couldn't get away from them anymore. So I turned the mother loose and she took care of it from there. They stay out in the woods all day long wandering around. She's training her pups. They come back all tucked out. I didn't feed them three times a day. In the morning and at night that's all.

I didn't had no sled, because that was the first dog team I had and I didn't know how to make sled. My dad told me how to make sleigh but he never did make sleigh for me. He told me what kind of birch to get and those things so I just start to use it. I had a family and I had to do it for myself then. I go out every day and cut birch and bring it home. October I got everything ready to put together. November our trapping season opens.

I went out with my brother-in-laws but I didn't use my dogs because I thought they were too young. They were four months old, ready to hook up but I didn't want to lose any of them. You can easily cripple a dog on clear ice. They're scared of ice. Mostly it's blowing down at 22 Mile. As fast as the snow come down it just blows away. There's nothing but just the clear ice out there. Even a human being can get hurt on it. Therefore, I didn't want to use my pups. So I just went with them on foot. They had nine dogs for their sled.

I'd start out in the morning and sometimes they'd never catch me up. As long as there was no more than a couple inches of snow on the ground I don't think anybody would keep up with me anyhow, even with dog team. The further I used to run, the more I like it. Seems like I'm just pretty light. I could almost float in the air the way I feel, when I start in running. We go down sixteen miles to our camp. Quite a ways out. They'd never catch me up even with their nine dogs. Sometimes they offer me a ride if they catch me up, I say no I'd rather walk. I'd rather run or walk. As long as there was a little snow on the ground I could run forty or fifty miles a day. I could run all the way to Nulato.

Run To Nulato

Christmas holidays a lot of people used to go up to Nulato for church and dances. One year I started out an hour after bunch of dog teams left. I was just about to cross the river when the first bell for school rang. Eight o'clock. I didn't have a watch or I would have kept my time. I never stop running. By 12 Mile I passed the second team. At 18 Mile lots of dog teams stopped for lunch. I didn't take no lunch. I was depending on these guys to give me a mouthful of tea, you know, to make it the rest of the way up. Edgar Kalland, he's my second cousin, offered a sandwich and some tea. After I ate I just left. It must have been about thirty or thirty-five below and all I had was a woolen shirt and gloves. It's good while I was moving but I couldn't sit around or all my sweat would frost up. I just ate my sandwich and left. All I carried was my snowshoes. After 18 Mile the trail goes across and then over on the other side. There I had a chance to be ahead of them. I went on the hillside all the way behind the island.

By the time I get up nine miles below Nulato, I see a whole string of dogteams way over on the other side. Edgar Kalland said he seen a guy about that big going across the Yukon way up there. Just like a bird going across the river. That was me. I get over the other side on the main trail and I met someone coming down from Nulato to meet one of their relatives. It was a good trail from there. He told me to ride. I said OK and sit on that sleigh for four miles. Boy! I couldn't move because my clothes all frosted up. I told him I got to walk. I couldn't sit on the sleigh. I might get too cold in the next two miles. So I start in running again.

That night there was a dance. I couldn't stay away from a dance. I had to go. We got in about four o'clock. I took a nap for about two hours and I start in dancing. I danced all night. Those days we used to have live music, violin and guitar. Lot of guys took turns playing for the dance. Everybody enjoy themselves and the dance would last till five or six o'clock in the morning.

Treat Each Other Good

My parents had an arranged marriage. Not like we do right now with paper marriage license and married by the church. Their folks put it together for them. They look for a guy who was a really good hunter or a good runner. A guy who would make a good living. If some young guy saw a girl, nice looking girl and they fall in love, well, that didn't go too far for the older people. They might think they'll never get along, never have a good home, or a good living. The most important thing the old people were thinking about in those days was to make a good living and have a good home for the daughter or son.

There's one story we joke one another about here in Kaltag. Long time ago a woman had a daughter. She was living alone with her daughter. No father

Photo by Jetté. Oregon Province Jesuit Archives

Old Man Madros, father of Jack and David Madros. Kaltag, circa 1919.

Photo by Jetté, circa 1919 in Nulato.

L-R: 1. Jack Madros, father of Florence Semaken, Jessie Sipary, Austin and Franklin 2. Little Peter 3. Kokrine Kriska 4. David Madros, Phillip's dad.

there. Pretty soon a young man came up the river and he wanted to marry this daughter. The woman told him to go across to a lake over there we call *Tomaats'a'oyh Dinh* to check her blackfish trap. She had trap for blackfish in that lake.

That man was gone long time, practically all day. Come back in the evening. Then he made a mistake. He said, "Gee that's long ways." But it wasn't very far. Evening went by and next day the old woman told her daughter, "You better tell that boy to go back down to his place. It looks like he isn't going to make a very good living the way it sounds."

Just these few words he said and the mother figured it out. It sounds like this is a lazy boy who wouldn't make a good living. They said some things like that. Parents look at the kids, look at each other, before the couple get together and stay with one another. But they found out it didn't always work. The parents might hear about a good worker they want for a son-in-law and force their daughter to marry him. They call that forced marriage. The way I see it forced marriage with somebody who doesn't love you doesn't work out.

I used to go around with my wife Florence ever since we were in school together. We got used to each other pretty much, but the one thing, our parents didn't like each other. Even so, they couldn't break our love between me and my wife. Florence was the same way. My parents couldn't break that love from her.

I had lot of other girl friends in other villages but it seems I wasn't going too much for them. In 1946 my parents were in Galena. I was down here in Kaltag because of Florence. Finally I went up to Galena and told my mother, "I'm going to get married."

"Well," she said, "How you going to feed your family?"

"I'll make out someway," I told her. She knew I was going around with Florence already. "Well," she said, "my son, if you going to get married, get married with somebody that don't drink, like you." That's all she said to me. Then I came down to Kaltag.

There was no marriage license or priest in Kaltag so I sent Florence up to Nulato. She went up and then I went up later with my brother's dogs. I stopped with Daniel Sipary, her sister's husband. He was really nice man.

I don't think there was any other better man than him. After we got married, we had a little party at his house. We said, "I'll go get somebody to talk to you. A guy who never left his wife even though he was drunk. Even he was drinking and his wife was drinking, I never hear that guy ever cuss at his wife at no time. I'm going to bring him tonight and while we eat he's going to talk to you."

So we sat down and then this guy was talking to me. He said, "I was married twice. My first wife, I really love her, and then she died. Now I got younger girl I'm married to. She drinks quite a bit. She runs around quite a bit. She had all the good times she can get. I never cuss at that woman or never lay my hands on her yet. And I hope you understand it well. You're getting married with a girl you love. You pick out the girl that you love." Just the way I was thinking he was explaining it to me. Then he said, "I hope you have a good living."

My grandma talked to me too in her own language. My wife was related to her so she said, "This girl is just like my daughter and she is the last, youngest one in this family. I think if you treat her good, she'll treat you good. You treat each other good and you'll make a good living. You'll have a good home."

Well, I listened to them and I talked to them and I realize what they're talking about. Later on I started to realize it a little bit more. Before she died this old lady come and asked me again. She said, "*Koy*, my grandchild. It's just like the way I told you when you was getting married. Just like you had a handful of what I told you and put it in your gloves. You're just doing it now." Then she started to get me a little bit more thinking about it.

I always thought if I'm not going to love a girl or if I'm not going to love my children and I start in drinking, I'll never get married. That's the way I figured. Even right now if I see a little kid like Goodwin Jr.'s boy, my heart is always moving with love for him. And not just that one, I've got four other grandchildren. They're all the same to me. They're just like one to me.

If they bother me, that's fine. I love it, because I love my grandchildren.

One summer I took my big boat up to Galena to pick up my daughters. They flew as far as Galena then I would bring them down. All four of the kids were small. Nice and quiet for awhile, sleeping. Then about forty miles up they all woke up. You know how kids are. They can't stay in one place. They run all over in the boat. Houseboat so I don't worry. I don't watch them all the time. Pretty soon they started in crawling all over me while I was driving the boat. All over my back and hang on my head. I never shout at them or anything. I think that they just love me like I love them.

Chapter Three: Subsistence Work

I didn't believe my father very much, but I started to think about myself. How am I going to make a living? I have to live off the country. That's the first thing that come into my mind. And then I had one little baby of my own. Here I couldn't get nothing fresh for her. There was no fresh food that I could buy for her. No fresh milk I could buy for her. I want a healthy family, so I just had to go out every day and kill something for her. Like fish or chicken or ptarmigan, rabbits, willow grouse, or whatever. Some little animal to keep my family healthy. I thought that would be the best thing that I could get for my kids. I had to go out and kill something fresh every day for them. My mother was the same way when she used to go out every day for us. I told my kids that.

Three Old Men and The Bears

There were some old guys like my uncle Slim Rubin and my uncle Alex Solomon, Sr. used to sit down and talk and talk about long time ago. And we used to sit and listen to them. Like me and Franklin Madros and Plasker Nickoli. We get interested in the guy that's telling us about things that we never seen. Things that maybe we have heard about but we hear it again. It was interesting just listening to those guys.

It was in August of the first year I was married we went hunting with three old guys. They asked if we want to go hunting with them. Me, and Simon and Missouri Stanley. This one guy had five-horse inboard gas boat. We used that to go down to 22 Mile. From there we went up on the hill. On the first hill we spotted a bear. These old guys tell us, "You and Simon go after that bear." Well, we were the youngest ones.

It was quite a distance off from where we were and already getting dark. I told Simon hurry up, let's go, so all we took was just our gun and our hunting knife and start in walking. I could walk fast and I could run fast. Most of the time I run, then walk. Run and walk trying to get to that bear. We get to the open place just as he was ready to call it a day. All day eating berries and he was ready to leave. We sneak out to it but it was open and we couldn't get too close. I told Simon, "You shoot first." He shot about a foot above the bear. I followed where he hit because the moss flew up. The bear kind of duck. He heard where the bullet hit and the shot from some other place. He stood and looked around. I shot and he jump up! Too low. He started running.

Usually a bear will go downhill when they run away from you. We keep shooting at it. I just took my good old time, shot, and pretty soon he roll over. I hit him right on the head! Mostly I call it an accident shot but I really took my time. I really wanted to get it. We butchered it right away, lay it down on willows and left. It was pretty dark already when we started back to where they said they were going to make camp.

Keep on walking. Walk and walk and walk. We were so much in a hurry going to the bear we didn't spot where we came from. Soon looks like we're kind of going in the wrong direction. We were going around a hill. We stop and listen, but we never fire a shot even though we didn't know where we were. Pretty soon we see a light way up on the hill. Simon's dad found out we were lost so he got up on the highest place and burned some birch bark to guide us back to camp.

Everytime you catch something like a bear it makes the old people happy. They know they're going to get something fresh to eat. Next morning when we got up they told us to go back and get the meat. Missouri and Robert Stanley went with us while the other guys made a cache. After they ate they said, "We're going further out. Out to the next hill."

I like that. Once I go out hunting I don't want to turn back. Even if I go out for one day, I don't want to come back till it gets dark. I was walking ahead down in the valley and up on the next hill. Missouri and Simon kept up but the old people were quite a ways behind. They could see our trail and they just keep coming. I spotted an open place on top of the hill and I wanted to come out there right away. I start to walk faster. Just when I was coming out in the trees, there was a bear out there. He never look at me, never heard me. He was too busy eating berries. I stopped. Those two guys came walking and I waved them to slow down. I show them the bear right out in the open eating.

All three of us get in line. I said, "I'm not going to shoot. I wait. You guys shoot." They shot and they shot the bear. We sit down and start talking. Pretty soon the three old men come. They skin it and we hang it up.

Next they want to go out on this big hill. They used to go out there when they were young they say and they all want to go out again. All three of them. Just to see the scenery again. We hang the meat up and we went up on

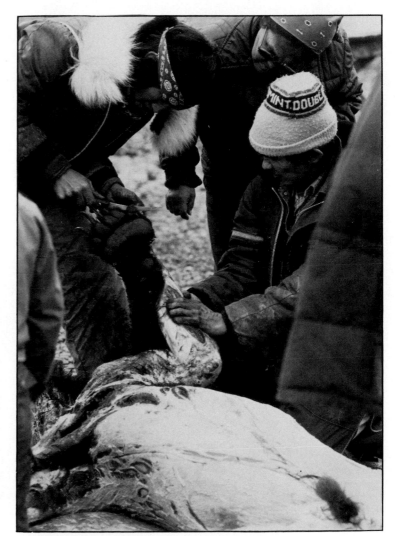

Floyd Saunders' family helps him skin his first brown bear on the beach at Kaltag, 1979. L-R: Tucker, Floyd, Raphael Neglaska

L-R: Floyd Saunders, Olga Solomon, Tucker

that hill. Then one of the old men said, "This is the place where we used to have camp. There's water close by here. We don't have to go down to the creek to get water. So we make camp right there. Then we started to go up higher. We stayed there all day. Next day we went back up there again. Gee lot of bears that time.

We were sitting on top of the hill and pretty soon we see two bears right at the foot of the hill. Two bears coming up the creek in an open place. We seen them.

The three old guys say they're going to those bears. We didn't say anything. There was Old Man Stanley, Missouri's dad, and Simon's dad. We stayed on the hill and watched. They went down the cliff and across that little

Andree Danteen

38

creek. On the other side of the creek was where the bear was. They were eating berries. Two big bears, two brothers.

We watched them come out of the willows. Just where the bear was, all three of them sneaking out. But they were all turning the wrong way! Where they seen the bear the last time, that's where they were sneaking out. But the bear moved further up. They were all sneaking the wrong way!

Missouri's dad came out first pointing his gun up the other way from the bears. These other two old men were right behind him. Then he stop and look around. He saw the bears and told the other two guys. From on top of the hill we could look almost straight down on them. We could see every move they make. We were making joke to one another about it. Pretty soon they up and shot. The first one drop. Shot again. Bang! Bang! The other one drop.

We took our pack, their pack, their knife, and went down to them. They skinned it. We didn't hang it up. We were going to bring it back to camp. Simon, Missouri and me were the young ones so we said we'll carry whatever we can, bring it to camp and divide it there. These three old guys say they'll pack what they can too, but the hill was pretty high.

Many years ago the people had been out there hunting caribou and bear. You could see their footprints just like steps all the way up the hill. These old guys told us where to find them. So we start in packing. Quite a ways up we took a rest. Big pack with those two bears. Another rest after that and we made it all the way up. But those old guys were still way down below half way yet. I tell them, "Let's go down and help them so they can come up empty-handed." I pick up my uncle's pack and this other old guy put his pack under my arm and then start walking up the hill again.

After they got on top of the hill they were happy. "Well," they said, "that's probably our last hunting. Probably that's our last animal we're going to kill." We had dinner and went to bed.

Next day it was raining, fog. You couldn't see nothing. We stayed under the tarp all day. Another day we stayed under there. Two days and a half we stayed under that tarp. We couldn't go any place. Raining, fog, couldn't see nothing. We know where to go all right, but it was too wet to travel. We just stayed. We had lot of bear meat, but nothing else. Just salt and bear meat. But that was enough for us. Bear meat and salt was the most important thing. We had no more tobacco, no more tea, no more sugar, no more bread. All we were eating was just bear meat. But we cook it different way every time. We hang it up in the smoke overnight. Next day maybe we'd boil it, or fry it, or whatever way we want. Then go eat some berries right around camp.

After two days and a half, the sun start to come in and out. So we start to go back. We were out there for nine days and we didn't know it. Nine days and we didn't even know the days were going by that fast. On the way we pick up the second bear and keep packing. When we got back on the hill where we had our first camp, we camp again. Next day it was raining again, but only two miles to go mostly downhill to our boat. It rained so hard we were all wet soaked through by the time we made it.

Four bears is a lot of meat to pack. No pack sack those days either. Just inch and a quarter webbing sewn to a sack. Some guys put a strap over their head to pull up the pack. Simon and me had to lift each other up to get on our feet. Once we get on our legs it is fine, but if we rest we have to help each other up again.

Down at the boat we put the tarp up and make a fire under it. Just start to sit around the fire and one of these old men is gone. After awhile he came back with some tobacco, sugar and tea. He knew we were going to run out of food on the hill so he hide some little of everything he had. When we come back, we'll have it here. After we eat they all smoke and chew. The rain never stop.

We put the tarp over the boat while the old guys sat around the campfire. After we were ready to go, we got in. The old men go up front. They were so happy they just start singing. They sing all the way up from 22 Mile. And the inboard goes slow. Three and a half hours singing and moving around. We could see them from where we sat behind the motor. Dancing, singing, moving around their body. They were so happy. All different Indian songs. Two of them were good singers. They know a lot of songs and make a lot of songs after loved ones they lost. We stop at their camp four miles below Kaltag, leave them and take their other boat the rest of the way home.

Hunting Moose

There wasn't much moose around here when I was growing up. I didn't see my first moose until I was 15. But there used to be caribou. They migrate over from the Innoko River through 22 Mile where my camp is. They only have one path to go over to the hillside when the snow gets deep. They cannot get enough food out there on the flat because there's too much snow. In the hills the snow isn't very deep because the wind keeps it blown off. Therefore they migrate across the river and get into the higher hills for their food.

Later on there started to be moose. If my dad saw one moose track, he'd get some guys from ten miles above us and twenty-five miles below us to get together. They all gather up to go after the moose. A whole bunch of them go after it. But they didn't know how to hunt it. No experience. They thought it was like caribou.

Those moose really make you work, but you got to keep going. When your family knows you're out, especially your wife knows you're out, they expect something out of you when you come back. Something fresh for the family. I always think of that. I don't want to come back skunked to my family. If I don't get anything I'll stay out there till I do. Those things come to my mind when I go out hunting, you know, when my kids were small.

I enjoy hunting alone. I can do whatver I want and I can sneak up on moose. But I like to go out hunting with some older guy, too. Even if I know what I'm doing and where I'm going, I never tell him. I always kind of depend upon the older guy to tell me. Lot of times I went out with my brother-in-law Clement. He's a good hunter and he's like me, he won't come back skunked. I know this country pretty good and I know where to go hunting, but I wouldn't tell him. I let him lead me. Tell me what to do and where to hunt, just to respect him.

Our parents used to tell us "Don't answer back to elder people. Maybe they got some experience behind them that they say something to you." That's why I get real mad if my kids answer me back. If I scold them and they answer me back, I blow my top. Because I never said that to my parents. My old man used to kick at me every morning. Used to give me hell every morning. I never said nothing to him because I always think my old man knows what he's talking about. It's experience he's learned he's explaining to me. I'm supposed to think about that. Realize what he is explaining to me.

Photo by Jetté in Nulato circa 1910. Oregon Province Jesuit Archives

L-R: Charlie Brush, Clement Esmailka, Wilson.

I killed a lot of moose, but I didn't do it for a pleasure. I did it to make a living for my family. And there is times moose used to make me really work. I always think that I should have listened more to the older people that knew how to hunt. They gather up all the old tracks and new tracks. They look at the branches the moose been eating and they can say how far away that moose is and when he is going to lay down. They hunt the easy way, but me,

I think I am a good runner. I could catch the animal anytime just running after it. If there's only little snow on the ground and hard for the animal then I'm careless hunting. I don't care if it's running away from me or it see me or smell me. I'm always pretty sure that I will catch it. Either I run it down or the animal give up. But a lot of times I get fooled that way too.

Clement Esmailka and me were chasing moose two and half days once. Good for us in snowshoes but deep snow for the moose. We both thought we would catch it easy. We chase it all day. Sometimes I could see it through the timbers or just its legs in the willows, but never close enough for a shot. I knocked off about 9 o'clock at night. Completely dark by then. Next morning we went after it again.

Pretty soon that thing start in spreading blood. He was overworking himself, cough out blood. Even at that I couldn't catch it. Even at that he was better than me. That night, dark again I thought Clement already went back to camp so I quit and made a short cut back. But Clement was still behind me. He was just walking steady. About 200 feet from where I turn off, that moose had just fell in a hole. Clement saw him jump up right in front of him. He tried to shoot at it a couple of times but it was too dark. Finally he ran out of shells and came back to camp.

Third morning again we went after it. This time we took a dog team to where we left off. We tracked them and I saw them just before they started to run. There were two. I start running after them but through the woods you cannot go very fast with snowshoes. A moose can go through faster because he can move around pretty good. In thick brushes you can't go very fast with snowshoes. In a place like that I seen him and he got away from me again. By the time I come out in the open I was going one direction and the moose went in the other direction. That way it fooled me. But my brother-in-law was right behind it. Tracking it. It came out in a lake and stopped right there. I passed it already and was about a mile up. I heard shots so I turned and came out near them. "Well, I got it," he said. "This thing really make us work."

Hunting on the Yukon. Photo from the Sisters of St. Ann's in Nulato circa 1930.

Well, we didn't have a choice. We had to go kill it. Regardless even though it was how many miles away from camp. We had to do it for our family. My brother-in-law already had three kids at that time. And my parents were old, so I had to go out and do something for them. They weren't able to go out and do whatever they used to do for us. It was our turn to do something for them then. I got six boys and five girls, eleven in my family right now. I watch him play basketball every night and I try to explain to him.

In the early days when I was growing up a lot of kids had a hard time making it. They get sick and die from lack of vitamins and vegetables. I didn't want to lose any of my family when I start to have family. The only thing I could think of was to go out and kill something for them every day. If I don't catch game, I had fishnet across the Yukon in the slough. Go out and catch some fresh fish. Something fresh. We had no fresh eggs, no fresh vegetables, and no fresh fruit. But there was something I could go out and kill for them. And the law didn't stop me. Regardless if there was a game warden in front of me I still would kill a moose. I'm doing it for my family. I'm not doing it for myself. I just wanted to have healthy kids. And right now I sure have healthy kids. Out of eleven I never lost any of my kids yet.

Honeymoon Slough

I know how my uncle Rubin was in his younger days, mostly out hunting the country. Hunting game all the time. Then he got pretty old and couldn't walk far anymore. He couldn't go trapping. So I asked him to go out hunting with me in my boat. He was happy to go. We stayed out for two days but we never even saw a moose. I walked back and caught a few geese. Then came back to him sitting at camp. Pretty soon George Madros and Franklin came down. They hunted with us for about a day, but we still didn't see anything. I sure didn't want to come back but I didn't have enough gas to go out any further. We went out the slough to the Yukon with them and there was a bunch of other guys on their way down to Honeymoon about sixty miles.

I wanted to go with them but I didn't have enough gas and no food. We ate all our food. I borrowed five gallons of gas from George. That would take me a long ways with my three horse Mercury. That's okay if I don't have food. I just want gas so I can run my motor. Then my uncle says he will go with me and we keep on going with those guys.

I never know the country down there and I want to see it. I figure that later if I don't catch anything in this area I could go down there and I'd know where to go.

Lot of moose tracks in the slough, Honeymoon Slough. Uncle sat up front and I was driving along the bank. Lot of fresh moose track. The other guys were quite a ways behind us so I was driving real slow. Then my uncle started to move around out there. He saw more fresh tracks because I was running real close to the beach. So I slow down the kicker little bit more just about idling. Then I seen a bull moose standing right on the bank. "Shoot the moose, Uncle! The moose up there!"

He grab his gun and shot. I could see where he hit. The willows fell down way high. I was ready too with my rifle. I shot and wounded it. I jumped off the boat, run up the bank and he was still standing. I shot again and got him. I hollered, "I got him, Uncle!"

"Thank you," he said.

Everytime they catch something, the old

Goodwin getting his gun from his cache. Kaltag 1982.

people are always happy. They know they're going to get something they have eaten before. They know how it tastes. Something fresh for them. We started skinning it. Pretty soon Plasker, Clement, and the rest came. We made camp right there.

Next day we went further and got couple more moose. We came back to out first camp and divided the meat up into the three boats. Next morning we came up the river. I don't know how long I was out, but like I said if I go out hunting I don't want to come back. As long as the weather is good I just want to keep on going. Sometimes I go just to see the scenery or see animals. If I got enough meat, I wouldn't kill anything. Just go see it, that's all. Even in these movies, if I see a movie about animals, I just sit there and watch it.

Back And Forth With Fish

When I get through with my sleigh in the spring I hang it up under the cache. I hang it upside down. Then my snowshoes the same way. I put them right on top of the sleigh to keep them out of the weather. If you just leave it out there in the grass it wouldn't last long. It stays wet all summer long and when you look for it in the fall you might even have a hard time to take it out of the grass. And that wood would rot. My dad used to tell me, "You have to buy everything when you start out but you wouldn't have money to do that every year."

I take care of my boats the same way over the winter. You can put them up on drums and keep the water and ice off of it so in the spring when you tip it back up it is just as dry as this floor. Then long as you paint it every year a wood boat would last a long time.

I thought a long time about getting ready for fishing. We used to wait till we could get our poles for the fish wheel and drying rack and cutting tables

Fish drying racks on the Kaltag riverbank.

with a boat. But that's a busy time. We have to be building the wheel and getting going on fish. So I get my poles on the crust the last part of April. Go way back along the creek and cut good ones. Haul them out with snow machine. I kind of figured it out to do it differently than other people. Now lots of people do that. We don't have to rush when the fish are running. Whenever I need some poles, I just go up to my pile on the bank put it in the boat and bring it to where I'm drying fish.

When they first came out with commercial fishing license about five or six years ago, people didn't understand it. That's why there's only eleven commercial fishing licenses in town. When it started all you had to do was apply for it. It cost about $20. Now you have to buy it from somebody for over $10,000 if anybody would sell it to you.

We used to go catch fish anytime we wanted, tonight, Saturday, Sunday, the whole week, or the whole summer. When commercial fishing came in you had to go by so many days open and so many days closed. Weather or storms didn't matter. It just went by the time and day of the week. Then they made it the same for subsistence. You have to pull your net and stop your wheel when it's closed. People didn't like it, but it's so fish will go by for the people upriver. I don't know why they limit us for kings. We never get good king salmon here anyway. The best we can catch is a few a day and they are about sixty pounds at the biggest. In the Rampart Rapids they get big ones. Lots of eighty to ninety pounders.

Summer of 1974 a guy came in here wanting to buy some roe. My brother Ottie had the only wheel going in town. I didn't want to put my wheel out then. It was ready to go but I still had it up the creek. I just bought fish for five cents apiece from Ottie for my dogs. So this guy who came down asked me to be a buyer for him. I said okay, because I wanted to help some people to get some more money. Pretty soon people started to put in more nets and

Goodwin securing his canoe to the roof of his boat.

Goodwin carrying a load to his boat in Kaltag.

I put out my wheel. I didn't know about having a fish license at that time. This guy brought down a form for me to fill out and then he brought down a license. That was the first commercial license.

The year after that my wife wanted one, too. I said, "Go ahead. Buy it. Then we'll have two." I tried to explain to the rest of the people but it seems like they didn't understand it. That was the only chance you had to buy a commercial license from the State. We have permanent ones but we have to renew them each year.

We were getting eighty-five cents a pound for roe that year. Everybody thought that was good pay. When I was growing up we used to sell dry fish for six cents a pound for sun-dry and eight cents a pound for smoked. We had to put up tons and tons of fish before we could make enough money for our winter supply of food. And it was a lot of work, too. I counted seven times you got to handle it before you get rid of it. First you take it out of your wheel and bring it back to camp. Throw it in a tub. That's twice. Then take it out of the tub, cut it and put in your container. From there you take it to your fish rack and hang it up. After a day you turn it around so both sides dry. When it's glazed, you bring it in the smokehouse. From the smokehouse you got to handle it two more times yet.

The trader here was the one who bought fish. Last one we had was Adolf Miller. He used to buy all the fish he could get. Even though he had enough he'd buy some more. He was just a man that tried to help the Natives. Pretty soon it'd take him a year or two before he'd get rid of them.

Even with selling fish, we didn't get enough to buy our winter grub straight out. In the fall when we get ready to go out trapping, the trader would give you all the groceries you want, up to so much. Whatever will take you till December. Then whatever fur you catch you bring back to him and he gives you the price for it. Then you pay your grocery bill. It just continues like that all winter long. Back and forth groceries for fur. Whatever you catch. Summertime we do the same thing with fish. Over and over, back and forth with fish. That way we were getting along pretty good till he died in 1937 and we had no store. Then we had to pay cash for groceries and go as far as Koyukuk or Unalakleet to get them.

Before Adolf died, the store had been going down a bit, but the worst thing, he didn't have no relatives. Nobody to back up that store. If he had relatives they would have closed that place as soon as he died and have everything straightened out according to the law. As it was, the people he was buying from Outside came in and just started grabbing stuff. Emptied that place right out. Now we have a Co-op store that's doing pretty good.

Storms

I had my wheel going down at 22 Mile and quite a bit of sun-dry fish on the racks there. I left my little boat with the twenty-horse kicker tied to a rock at camp. I came up to town and then a strong south wind with rain came up. I didn't have a chance to go down and check it. Lucky I didn't tie the boat to something that would hold it there. Instead the wind blew it upriver dragging the rock. There it was when I went down. Hardly even any water in it. I thought for sure that storm would swamp it.

Then I stayed in town for awhile. Pretty soon here comes another storm. I lost my wheel, my boat, kicker and all. I thought and studied it for a long time. Then I got my nephew's boat and enough gas to go all the way to Grayling looking for the boat. There's a place below my camp that things always stop. So I ran close to the beach. Soon it looked like there was a log back there. But the log looked pretty straight. No kicker, though. I figured that kicker would be sticking up if the boat was upside down. But sure enough it was the boat upside down. The kicker tilted so you couldn't see it. I told my boy, "I don't know whether we can get it out."

We went back to camp, got my hip boots, and walked in the water. No way I can turn it up. We went back again and got rope and come-along. We could only turn it up so far then it went back down. So I just took off my top clothes, went under and unscrewed the kicker. It was buried in the mud and that's why we couldn't tip the boat up. Then we could get the boat up about half-way. I walked out and put a pole under it to hold it. We slacked back the come-along and got another bite on it. We got it all the way over, but it was full of water. First we tried bailing it, but then I got an idea. I tied it to the back of my boat, pulled the drain plug, speeded up my kicker and drained all the water out on the way back to camp. When we got to camp it was floating on top of the water.

I brought the kicker up to town and took it all apart. I thought it would never run again. Every bolt came out to dry and get washed in oil. Then I let it sit for a couple days. I began to get lazy to put it back together again so I asked Freddie Alexie. He did it. Just pulled the rope and it started.

That same storm floated away my wheel. The cable didn't break, it came apart in the connection. So I asked Father Sebesta to fly me down to look around for the wheel. I took Franklin and Plasker with me for the ride. I paid Father anyway for the gas. He wouldn't charge as long as we pay for the gas. We found the wheel fifty miles down on a bar. Quite a ways to haul a wheel — fifty miles. I thought I should bring down two boats, get the baskets and let the raft go.

Well, then I began to think how long it took me to make that raft. Two days to make it but only six hours to bring it back up. Plus sixty gallons of gas. Next day we went down with my son's fifty-horse, my nephew's fifty-horse, and my twenty-horse. It came up pretty good. All the way in four and half hours with three boats pushing. We brought it all the way and put it in the slough. I figured it out so I did it all in one day instead of three or four days making a new raft next season.

Chapter Four: Unalakleet

Wolverine Trade

Before riverboats, must be in the 1870's, people from way upriver used to go to Unalakleet to get groceries. Nulato, Koyukuk, even as far as Tanana, people used to come downriver to go over the portage to Unalakleet. By 1900 the miners started coming upriver and steamboats brought groceries along with the supplies. But Slim Rubin, John Chiroskey and us still went to Unalakleet. Ships from Seattle couldn't get into the bay at Unalakleet because it was too shallow so they stopped at St. Michael sixty miles south of there.

Later on they started to talk about the railroad from Seward to Fairbanks. All those steel rails came up the Yukon on sternwheelers. After 1928 we got our groceries coming down the river from Nenana, everything turned around again.

Besides just groceries we used to go over to Unalakleet for visits. A lot of people knew my parents and they'd give them some of their Eskimo food. My mother had to have some Eskimo food mostly all the time. I grew up on it, too. Right now I don't really care much for Eskimo food but I still got some, like seal meat or seal oil. I got some seal oil in my refrigerator right now. If I don't have it then I'll want it. I'll want it every day. But as long as I got it here, then I don't think about it.

Last fall some Eskimos came over and they brought a whole seal for me. "Goodwin, I brought you a seal. You can do whatever you want to do with it." He had it all cut up in a bucket. "You can pass it around or you can have it all."

"Well," I tell him, "That's too much for me. As long as I got a little bit,

I'm all right." So I just went around town and gave some to different people. A lot of people like seal oil or whale blubber very much in here. If it's whale blubber I'll eat that every day. As long as I got it. But seal oil, I don't go too much on it. If there's cooked blubber I could eat that for breakfast and supper.

We always keep going over to Unalakleet. Even after we had a store here my parents would go over there with some few beaver skins or marten skins, whatever they don't sell to the store. Used to be a real good market for wolverine skins in Unalakleet. You can almost get a young girl for a wolverine hide. That's how much they want wolverine skin in those days. That reminds me of another story about the place my mother was raised *K'inaakkoy Nuggut*, Reindeer Station in English.

There was one man living there, well-off man. They call him a rich man, you know. And he had a daughter. A lot of different young guys that go by there want that daughter. But this old guy don't want to give his daughter away. Maybe he didn't know these young guys real well, or maybe he already knew something about them and he didn't want to give his daughter to anyone.

So this old guy was coming through there and he knew where this rich guy had set for wolverines. Wolverine is the biggest important thing around here in those days. If you see it in somebody's trap and you kill it, you got to come to that guy with the news. You say, "You got wolverine in your trap. I killed it for you."

"Well," he'd say, "what you want?" But he meant whatever you want to the guy who brought the news.

So this guy was coming through and he knew where this rich man had a set for wolverine. Just for some purpose he went by that trap and there was wolverine in there. Us people, like I say, tease one another about it, you know. There was wolverine in there, so he went back right away to *K'inaakkoy Nugguy* and told this guy. "There's wolverine in your trap back there.'' Must be some deadfall trap that they set long ago.

"Well," he asked him, "What that woverine said to you?"

"He said, 'In years ahead there's going to be somebody to work at your boots for you' ". He wanted this rich man's daughter but he explain it that way to him. He said there'll be somebody working at clothes for him. That guy knew right away what he meant so he gave him his daughter.

Whatever that woverine said you cannot pass it. It just has to be done. This guy had that in mind. He wanted to get his daughter before, but the old man wouldn't give her out. So he figured it out and checked his trap. With the wolverine in there he's sure he's going to get what he wants, no questions asked.

Trip To Unalakleet

Not too far back when we didn't have a store in here we used to go over to Unalakleet for groceries. Even now the manager of the store over there, half-Eskimo man, knows me real well. Regardless if it's Saturday or Sunday he'll open the store for me. Last summer I wanted to get a kicker and some groceries so I made a trip over. My two nieces were staying with me at fish camp so they went with me, Marylene Esmailka and Josephine Semaken. Josephine is married to my nephew so she is my neice but I think of her just like my daughter. As long as she is with me I don't have to think about cooking or washing my clothes and everything like that.

Eleven o'clock at night when we got there by plane with Ryan Air Service, I know a lot of them are already in bed. But I went to a dealer I know. He wasn't there, only his son was there. So his son called him up in Anchorage to say I was there to get a kicker. Turns out he didn't have the size I wanted so we went over to the A.C. store. On the way we saw Frieda Reilly going into her smokehouse. She just drop what she got and run over to hug me.

"When did you come over?"

"Just now. We came over to do a little shopping but the stores are closed," I told her. I brought my two nieces in her house for tea and we sat around and talk for awhile.

Pretty soon her husband Nickoli got out of bed and started talking with me. "If you got no place to stay, come back. We'll make room for you."

"I'm going over to Richard Ivanoff. See if he got a phone, then I'm going to call up my buddy, his brother Roland." I went over there and they were drinking. I didn't know they were. I never would have gone in there if I'd known they were drinking. Richard already passed out, only his wife answered the door. "Goodwin! You came!" She hugged me. "Yeah, we just come in. I was wondering if you had a phone. I want to call up Roland see if we could stop with him tonight. I know they're in bed by now." She told me to come in, then backed up against the door. "Goodwin, you're not going out. You're going to stop here with us."

They know Marylene but it is Josephine's first trip so I introduce her. Then her husband heard my voice even though he was passed out. He jumped up. "Goodwin, you came! I quit drinking right now, my friend. Right now I won't take any more drink. I know you never drink. We're going to eat." She started to cut up some meat, but they know I want Eskimo food. "Margie," he called his wife, "go get some berries for Goodwin. Fish or seal oil. Whatever he wants." Then he open up the refrigerator and ask what I want. That's how much those guys respect me. We had some berries, salmon strips and fish. Then we talk and talk for about an hour. Pretty soon they sober up and insist that we stop with them. "We got four beds in there empty right now. All my kids are out. You take one room and these two ladies will take another room."

Next day was Sunday. I found Martin Nanak manager of the AC store and mentioned that we came over to do a little shopping. He said, "OK, Goodwin, I'll open the store for you." I bought two fifty-horse Evinrude kickers and Josephine picked out five boxes of groceries. Martin got a truck to haul it all up to the airport. Boyuk was there.

We were set to go out with Boyuk, he's manager and pilot for Ryan Air Service, at two o'clock. I told him we had quite a bit of stuff and probably no room for the kickers. "Don't worry about the kickers," he said, "because we're going to make a run down to Kaltag for fish eggs for the Japanese. We'll put those kickers on that plane and it won't cost you a penny. We left that day and the next day they sent the kickers over.

Lost On The Tundra

It's ninety miles to Unalakleet and I know every mile. One March a bunch of us were going over for groceries. My brother Michael and Walter Andre left nine o'clock in the morning. Austin Esmailka kind of waited for me and left at two o'clock. I got off work at 4:30 and left by five o'clock. I had fourteen-horse Polaris snowmachine so I thought I could catch him up on the trail.

I left driving along pretty fast. Past 22 Mile I caught up to Austin and his father-in-law. I told him I know every mile of this trail, but I followed Michael's trail and pretty soon I got lost. I didn't even know where I was. At 10 Mile I saw a light way down in the open place, open flat. I went straight to them and asked them what they were doing. They said they were lost. They didn't know where the trail was.

Well I know exactly where the trail was, me, you know. "I'll go ahead of you," I said. "There's new trail up here past Pete's Camp. The old trail is out here, just where those cottonwood are. Let's go up to Pete's Camp. If there's no trail there maybe we'll stop overnight.

So I went ahead of them. Sure enough there was trail there. We didn't even stop. Just kept right on going. I know all the way, you know. I led them to Old Woman. From Old Woman it's all mostly open country. I don't think we followed the trail. One of my buddies was with me standing on the sled. We were riding along and pretty soon he seen a light way out there at the White Alice station. Used to be the army communication system. That White Alice was fourteen miles this side of Unalakleet. We could see the light off and on, but the weather was closing in. Snowing and blowing. Once in a while you couldn't see it. I

Out on the trail to Unalakleet.

thought I was going straight all the time. I went down towards the creek. I don't know how I turned around. I don't know how I made a big circle. I was driving along. Never looked back for those other guys. There were three other snow machines behind me. I never looked back. Pretty soon I seen fresh trail right in front of me and I stopped there. I turn around to my friend. "Oh boy! Trail to Unalakleet now." I tell him.

"That's our trail," he said.

"Our trail?" I ask him.

He walk up to me and said, "You made a big circle and then come back. I was wondering what you was doing."

These other guys caught me up. Austin asked, "Why'd you make a big circle for?"

"I didn't know it. I thought I was going straight." So I tell them to go ahead of me. I kind of recognize the place where we were then. I told them

58

go right straight up there and then you'll hit those tripods. Every mile across the open country they had a tripod set up. I started to drive behind them.

Pretty soon they stop and I catch them up. They want to drink tea. We look at the time. It was two o'clock in the morning. Might as well camp so we'll get an early start. "Let's go up in that valley and make camp. It was really dark and we couldn't see the light again at White Alice. We stopped, made camp, and went to bed.

It was getting daylight about eight o'clock. My brother-in-law got up and made fire. I looked around. When I looked down towards the Unalakleet River I knew where we were. Exactly where we were. I said, "We're twenty-three miles away from Unalakleet and the Whaleback is right down in here."

After we ate breakfast, we all left. I got behind them. They were all driving fast. Pretty soon I see them way out there by a little creek going into the Unalakleet River. They call it the Chiroskey River. I thought they were lost again. I just took my time going down to them. "Where's the trail?"

I looked. "Gee, I think it's down this way." I guessed right that time. I didn't know where the trail was exactly. I think it's down this way. All open country. We kept on going. Pretty soon I recognized the place where the trail crossed the Chiroskey River. They started to go ahead of me again. They open up their motors.

Pretty soon I started to catch them one by one. Driving too hard their motors got too hot. Going with the wind. Everytime you go with the wind with snowmachine it gets really hot. Finally we got to Unalakleet. Things like that can happen on the tundra. You can get lost. But out in the woods is worse.

Chapter Five: Making A Living

Steamboat

When I was 10 or 12 I helped my parents cut steamboat wood. That was the only income they had, cutting wood for the boat. My dad got six dollars a cord for it. We cut fifty to seventy cords in the falltime before trapping. A lot of guys my age did that. Some get their whole winter outfit that way.

Later on I worked on the Steamer *Nenana*. They got it in a park in Fairbanks now. I worked two months on that boat and then I could get groceries from the government commissary real cheap. I could get 200 pounds of flour and tea, sugar and lard. Things that we used quite a bit. I got those by the case and still it didn't run up over $70. We were getting about $140 a month.

When I first started I was a deckhand, then they put me on deck boy. I don't know why, because I was really enjoying my job with the deckhands. I had to get up at five o'clock in the morning and clean up the captain's house, all the bathrooms and the officers' kitchen. Mop it up and mop the deck. That takes three or four hours then I got nothing else to do all day.

Everytime we get to a woodpile to pick up I go help the deckhands for something to do. Haul some wood or take someone's place passing wood. The firemen had to have somebody to pass wood to. Sometimes I sit there for five hours passing wood, just helping these other guys. That way people begin to like me. I get more friends. I got really acquainted with the deckhands. I'm supposed to be around the captain's house most of the time but I don't do it. Once in a while he'd ring the bell and I'd run up there for whatever he wants.

When we get to Nenana, I never think about drinking. The rest of the deckhands go uptown, get drunk. Then when they're supposed to be working in the morning, they're gone. I never even go up around the village. I'd go around a bar and play pool for a little while then go right back down to the boat because I like to gamble too much. If I go to Fairbanks or Anchorage right now that's where I'd be hanging out, playing pan or blackjack. I never play heavy. No heavy games. Just probably twenty-five cents a chip or nickle a game. I could enjoy that more than going around in the bars getting drunk.

After the season on Steamer *Nenana,* I stayed in Galena with my parents and went to work for the Army building the airstrip. I really enjoyed that job all winter. We had a house in the old village. I used to run all the way around the dike and up to the hanger. Sometimes I pass it and go around again just to run. It seems like the further I run the better I like it. Sometimes I speed up. Run with all I got and still never puff.

My job was mostly clean up and move things around. You know how the Army is. Always moving things here and there. If you move something over there, maybe next day you'll have to move it back. That's the way the Army is.

I learned how to drive a truck there at the same time. I was working with one soldier who was our truck driver. I used to drive the truck for him. He'd sit by me. I'm not supposed to drive as long as I wasn't in the Army. But no officers catch us.

School

I always figure that if I get married I want to be by my wife. So I never went to the cannery or out firefighting like other guys from here. Nineteen fifty-six I got a job with BIA at the school. Ten years later they sent me to maintenance school at Mt. Edgecumbe in the month of July. It was supposed to be five weeks but the fish were running so they let us go a week early. Eleven of us were there from different villages. I didn't have much school, just up to the third grade, but I had a lot of experience behind me. I really enjoyed that school. I learned a little mechanical, carpentry, how to cut tins and how to wire electricity. Furnaces, boiler, water, and sewer. I learn how to take care of all those things and I'm still using it yet.

The next year we went for five more weeks. Eight hours a day till five o'clock. But when I go to bed I can't sleep. Sit in a classroom eight hours a day and no work. Just look at books and listen to a guy. Not enough work to put me to sleep. I get to sleep about two o'clock and six o'clock I'm wide awake. Four hours of sleep every night. I walk around for awhile, then go down to the mess hall, I couldn't sleep no more. And I feel just fresh. No work, not tired. I was glad to be learning. I was going to use that for my future. I miss my family but five weeks is not long.

I use that schooling a lot. Whenever anything breaks down I have to fix it. This winter all the furnaces went out. My oldest brother died in Nulato so I had the week off to go for the funeral. I told Mr. Kyle, the principal, if anything goes wrong call me up, maybe I could explain it over the phone. Well, the furnaces went out and Mr. Kyle and Glenn Olsen were on the phone all night long. I was telling them what to do. They were doing it and the furnaces never came on. Me and Henry Ekada stand by the phone up there all night. I never thought about those two switches.

Finally they couldn't get it going and the school building was getting cold. Harold Esmailka was there too for the funeral. I went over to him to ask if he could bring me down with his plane. It was pretty cold. He didn't think he could get it to start. It was two o'clock in the morning. I told Henry I got to get down there some way before the school get too cold.

Father Sebesta just flew in from some other place that evening so his plane was still pretty warm. I went down and woke him up. We got on the plane and flew down. About two-thirty we got here and start in working at the furnace. Father was with us all during that time looking at the blueprint. Pretty soon he found out that there are some switches someplace that cut it off. Then I thought of the switches. There was an AVEC electrician here too and he couldn't figure out what was wrong. We jumped a wire to get one furnace going just enough to keep the school warm. Finally at four o'clock I came down there and turned on the switches and all the furnaces start in working.

I told Henry let's go to sleep. We just lay on top of the bean bag and went to sleep right there.

My dad used to go up to Nulato to pick up the mail, get just a couple hours sleep and turn around. He caught up on sleep in Kaltag. I'm the same way. If I go up there and play poker all night, I can come down, sleep for twenty minutes and I'm good for another eight hours. As long as I keep moving I never get sleepy. As long as I'm working I never even feel it. I can work till I drop the way I feel. I think my age is catching up with me now and I start to feel it now if I get lack of sleep. But if I got something to do pretty steady I can do it till I'm done with that work. After that then I could sleep. If I sit down I could sleep. I could just sit down on the chair and sleep for half an hour sitting up. Then I got enough sleep again for next ten or twelve hours.

TB

I kind of hurt myself trying to make a living for my family. I got down with TB in '48. I thought for sure I was going to die. I couldn't get up any more.

I went to the hospital in Seward and the doctor said I had a little spot on my lung about the size of a fifty cents piece. "It's not very deep," he said, "and it's not very serious but you can take the cure if you try." I had a family of three at the time already. Three kids and I thought it was better if I go to hospital and stay there instead of spread that disease to my young ones.

So I stayed in the hospital for twenty-two months. Just stayed there and done everything what the doctors and the nurses told me to do. They couldn't give me any kinds of treatment. They said it's up to me to get cured. They were thinking about surgery on me but the spot was too small to do surgery. They tried some drug called INH but I was allergic to it. There wasn't very much drug those days for TB. So I just stayed in bed. Never get out of bed for three full months. I just lay on my back and try to take all the rest I could take.

After three months they took my x-ray. I had improved a little bit so I could get up and exercise. Sit up, go to bathroom, go get my own tray. I did that for the next three months until my next x-ray. They checked for TB germs in my sputum, too, but it was always negative.

This place was the Seward Sanitorium, an Army hospital. They used the place mostly for surgery and since I didn't need surgery they asked if I wanted to transfer to Juneau or Sitka. But I thought that was getting a little too far away from my family. I was already far away. The doctor said it was up to me. They don't try to buck the patient at that time. They try to make the patient happy so he can get well.

After nine months they let me walk around and do whatever I wanted to do. But I was still taking orders from the doctor. Then they started to show movies for the patients. I got to wheel the projector around on a cart to the four wards. There were two men's and two women's and one children's ward. I couldn't go in the children's ward but I got to go to the others. That way I got to know all the patients in the hospital. Then the nurses used to tell us to have a pen pal. Write to one of the other patients. So we have somebody to write to or talk to or go visit. Nurses used to deliver our letters for us to the next patient.

There's quite a few guys died with tuberculosis, here in Kaltag. Most of them have no business with the disease. Most of them just overworked themselves. That happened to me, I over did myself. I was just trying to make a living for my kids. I have to go out spring hunting for my family and I know there was a time when I couldn't even lift up my canoe to walk through a portage. But I just lift that thing up and put it on my shoulder.

Besides the canoe I have all the ducks and muskrats, whatever I catch, plus my guns. I have to carry that maybe a hundred yards. I can't even bend down. I just drop my canoe right off my shoulder. That's how tired I used to get. That fall I had a hemorrhage.

Other guys did that too. They used to carry their canoes from over on the other side of the West Hills. Some guys much stronger and healthier than me have died with TB because they overworked themselves. I think about all those things.

Drinking

I listened to my dad quite a bit when I was growing up. He used to scold us every morning. I had six other brothers in the same house. Not like the house we got right now. No rooms. Just a small little house, probably twenty-four-by-thirty-feet with six of us in there. My dad used to get up early in the morning and scold us because we sleep too long. He said we should be going out cutting wood, running around. Have exercise, or just move around in the woods out there. I started to think more about it. All my brothers were drinking so he was a little bit harder on them than me because I never drank. I never drank all my life.

Then my mother used to cry to me, "Don't drink. Don't drink." She never used to drink or smoke or use tobacco. "Don't drink, my son," she used to tell me. After I got married I began to think that way about my children. I began to think I don't need to drink. I got a family that made me happy. There's nothing better than my family. There's nothing in the world that's going to beat my family. I love my family. So then I decided I don't need to drink. I'm having just as much fun as guys that drink. In fact I got more fun than them. I know what's going on. Some people that goes to Nulato for Christmas holidays, Stickdance, potlatch, or dog race. Some of them don't even see it. They just go up there, get drunk, stay drunk for a couple days, and come back down. Then they ask you a question, "What was going on in Nulato?"

Lots of pressure to drink. People start in drinking and then they want to go see their buddy. Start in giving drink to one another. Well, there's a lot of other things that you could give your buddy. You don't have to drink to have a buddy. But that's the way most people think. The greatest thing right now is a drink, to meet your buddy with a drink. I never think that way yet in my life. I mean if I had a buddy that's drinking, I don't think I'd be too happy to give him a drink. I'd be real happy to take him to a restaurant or some other place where I could feed him. Drinking doesn't mean that much to me to make a good friend.

Boy I was tickled when Kaltag passed that law against liquor this winter. Seems like it was pretty good for awhile. Everybody follow the rules pretty good. I was so proud of it, I even tell guys in Anchorage. Seems like it was quieting down quite a bit. My son is on the City Council and he was hitting real hard on it even though he likes to drink.

I had to go over there and tell him, "You got two kids, two little boys there. How you guys are drinking when you got two little kids? That's the best thing you're ever going to have. Those two little boys right there. The best thing you're going to have while you're living. You never think about that? I didn't bring you up like that." My daughter-in-law was sitting down by me just crying. I said, "I never brought you up like that. If your mother was living right now you'd never touch those two kids. I'd take them away everytime you drink. Then you'd think about those kids. I never brought no kinds of liquor in my house to teach you how to drink. I always try to bring something that's good for your health."

Last fall I brought one case of beer and put it right by my steps in my house. My boys come and ask me, "Can we borrow a six-pack, Daddy?" I told them, "No, when I'm ready I'll tell you." Then I got my daughter and daughter-in-law to cook a big supper and invite everybody, Junior and his wife, Harold Semaken and his wife. We're going to have a big party I tell them.

We sat around the table and then I opened the case of beer. "Okay, help yourself now, you boys. I never brought anything like this for you boys in here, not even once while you kids are growing up. But now I'm going to tell you. Junior," I tell him, "You got two nice boys, two heartbreaking kids. I don't think there's nothing better than those two little kids in this world. That's just the way I thought of you when you was growing up. Now both of you drink once in awhile. I never drank all my life, but I thought, one of these days if I start in drinking, I'm not going to stay around my family. I know your mother never used to like drinking. I don't blame her. Her parents used to drink quite a bit. I thought as long as I start to have kids, I'll never touch anything like that. I'm still thinking that way right now. So if you guys quit drinking I'll feel real good."

I try to teach my boys how to do things like trapping or making fish wheel, or building a house. I tell them, "If you try one of those things I'm 100% behind you. If you try for yourself. Try to make something out of yourself. But if you want to drink, I cannot tell you to quit drinking. It's just like if you get around my table and want to eat and I say to get off my table I don't want to feed you. That'd be the same thing. So I cannot tell you to quit drinking. Not one of you can I tell to quit drinking. But if you start in drinking don't let the bottle be the boss of you. You buy the bottle and you're the boss of the bottle. If the bottle is handling you, that's the time to quit. That's the time to lay off." I got those things figured out. If I start in drinking, the bottle won't push me around. I buy the bottle and I'm boss of the bottle.

Fire

When ASHA came in here making houses, we got running water. Then we all had to have a water heater. Instead of buying one from ASHA, I got one from Standard Oil, which is Chevron now. I didn't have the right kind of connection on it to get enough draft. It was going to be too long a chimney in my two story house so I just connect it onto my oil stove. That's how it soot up. I didn't know it soot up and that's how it exploded.

I couldn't think at the time because it went up so fast. All I had to do is just turn on the water and spray the water on that water heater. And I had the oil expansion tank in the house. Five gallon is all I was using. If I'd had a drum outdoors it wouldn't have exploded.

My wife and kids just come back from church and were playing outdoors. I was uptown visiting some guys there. My wife run out. Another woman who was visiting run out. I run down and the house was just full of smoke already. Then my wife start in crying. I said, "That's okay. Let it burn down. Couldn't do nothing with it. We couldn't stop it." All the people from the village came and tried. Used all their fire extinguishers and couldn't get it out. I just told them, "Let it go. Let it burn down. I'll build another one. I'm strong yet."

I called Galena Air Service, Norm Yeager. "You want to come down and pick up my family? My house burned down." He said, "Okay, Goodwin, I'll come down." He sent down a 207. Took all my kids to Galena. From there I made reservations for Alaska Central Air to take them to Fairbanks to stay with my daughter. They went to school there for two weeks. I came back down and tear down everything that was left. I just tear it all down.

There was one lady here that had empty house. She said we could live in there until we build another one. It was a pretty good size building, but still too small for my family. Then some of my friends in Fairbanks took me out to where they were selling second hand furniture at auction. Somehow this guy running the auction found out that my house burned down and I need furniture. He was kind of helping me, too. He was cutting down the price on every one before he went too high. So that way I got all the furniture. Then I flew it all down on a plane. People really help me out. Galena Air Service came down and picked my family up for nothing. Just to make a run to help me out. And Alaska Central Air flew them on to Fairbanks for nothing. I got quite a help from different places.

Goodwin's two-story house and caches.

69

PHS was here then putting in the sewers. I asked the foreman if I could use the Cat to get some logs for myself. He said fine, so I wandered around back there and found a place where I could get all the logs I needed. Nice good logs. Nobody cut logs there before. People just offer to go back and cut logs for me. They don't want to get paid. So I brought down four cases of beer and told them to take that thing back there and cut some logs for me. One night they cut eighty logs all ready to haul out. Next day they got twenty more. That's

Spring break-up on the Kaltag riverbank. L-R: Junior Solomon, Goodwin Sr., Austin Esmailka

enough help right there for me. I could haul them out with Cat.

Springtime the ice pretty near melting. Austin offered to make the road for me and I drive the Cat with four loads each night. It took me four nights to haul out 120 logs. I was working in the school in the daytime. Very little sleep I was getting, but I was enjoying my work too. I started to build the house.

I figured I had to have a foundation. Most people put their logs right on the ground. But we have permafrost here and every house like that, the floor goes down in the middle. Logs right down on the ground heat up the ground from the house and it thaws out. It makes the house slack down in the middle and if the logs are not getting air they're just rotting away. I filled barrels up with gravel and set them down on the permafrost. I had to make my own transit to do it. I put a level down quite a ways off and aimed those barrels up and down. Some places I had to use a ice pick to put the drums down even with the other drums. It took me pretty near all summer. Go over there and dig out a shovel full every day. Toss out about an inch or inch and a half every day. Put the drums down even. That house would never settle an inch.

Summertime we had a Youth Corps program here. I asked the coordinator if I could teach these boys how to build a house. They said go ahead so I tell them what to do, how to put the logs and we go up about ten logs high.

Then it was too high for those kids so I got some people to build it for me.

Kaltag's octagonal community hall in the center.

I got all the blueprint in my head. I eat lunch quick and help for an hour in the day, then go at it at night till two or three o'clock in the morning. Roof and all on by November. December we moved in. I really put some work into it. But it seems like it didn't bother me too much. As long as you're working everyday I think it wouldn't bother me. But right now looks like I kind of slacked down on my work lately. Kind of slow down even though I could do it. I don't know why, guess I figure I got nobody to do it for. But I still got my kids to think about yet. Especially my two young girls that are still in school right now.

Community Hall

We've got a good community hall now but we had to fight to get enough money to build it. When I was on City Council I started to think about that kind of place. The State only gave us $2800. I know that's not even enough to get started on. And then people wanted to get forty and sixty foot logs for a big place. I know that's going to be pretty hard to get and take a lot of time. That long of logs takes a lot of man power, too. I thought how about an eight corner or six corner building and use twenty-four foot logs. You can pick twenty-four foot logs anywhere.

We could buy some gas and give a few dollars to young guys and go cut some logs. A six or eight corner building would be bigger than forty-by-sixty-foot anyway. They didn't know how they were going to do it or who was going to do it. After awhile I took seventeen guys up to 18 Mile and showed them the logs. It took them one week to cut 160 logs. Gee I got mad. 'Cause when I lost my house in fire we went back and cut 80 logs one night and they were all 40 foot logs. They were much harder to handle than 24 foot logs. And only 10 of us. There were 17 of them. They were making home brew and having parties and everything. I found out about it three or four days later. When they finally brought the logs down they left forty or fifty up there.

That summer the Youth Corps start. I went up with them and we spent twelve hours getting the logs out and getting down here. I knew it was going to be hard pulling logs up the bank with only little kids but we did it. We dug trenches down and started to pull the logs up. Some ladies went by and they start in pulling logs up with us.

Then we asked some construction guys building the school if they would haul some gravel for me. I wanted to put the whole community hall on a pad of gravel. We couldn't get that much gravel so instead I pick up all the drums around town. We filled the drums with gravel and sink them into the ground down to permafrost. These kids were doing it, Youth Corps. And they were doing it right.

Pretty soon we run out of money. It was like that for two years. Fighting for some money. Try to build that place up. We had all the logs already. Then they told me to figure up how much material we would need to finish it. We came up with $12,000 worth of material and $30,000 worth of labor.

They asked how we're going to put on that top. I said, "We'll figure out some way how we're going to do it." Even though I never figure up anything. I just designed the floor pattern that's all. I said, "Some carpenters will take care of it." Plasker took over from there. When they start building, that's all he was doing just making a blueprint of his own.

I was working at the school and just go up there once in awhile to see how it was going. Nineteen days and that place was up. They were really going. Twenty, all working like mad men. When they were done we had 2,600 square feet inside. We've got a wood stove, barrel stove, in there but I tried to get them to buy a oil furnace like the school's.

Goodwin approaches the community hall with a covered dish for Stickdance festivities, April 1983.

Inside the community hall, April, 1983.

Goodwin giving a speech at the 1983 Stickdance potlatch.

Singers at the Stickdance in Kaltag, April 1983. L-R: Goodwin with sticks, Clement Esmailka, Tassie Saunders, Maryetta Neglaska, Madeline Solomon, Mary Vent.

76

Dancing around the stick at about 10:00 p.m.

Dancing at midnight and hanging furs on the stick.

6:30 a.m. as dancing continues around the stick as the morning sun lights the cupola windows.

Youth Corps

The first year they had the Youth Corps I volunteered to supervise them. We had about 10 young teenagers. It wasn't very much of a program but it was for kids to teach them how to work, like go to work on time, never answer their boss, no smart remarks. We just clean up the village, cut grass and pick up trash.

Second year I began to think a little more about it. After we finished cleanup we had lot of money left over. They didn't know what to do with it so they told me to hire everybody between 9 and 20. I got forty-nine kids. That's why I'm so gray now. I couldn't find jobs for all of them. I started to think a little more.

Pretty soon I divided them up into six groups, eight or nine kids in a group and one of them as boss. One group was for teaching the young ones how to play baseball. All the girls start to show one another how to bake. The women's club let us use their building. It had a propane stove and all the cooking utensils ready to go. Some other boys I took back in the woods and cut out a place for a picnic ground. The other crews I told to haul gravel along the road in place of the boardwalks. The boardwalks were too old and not any good anymore. All of them started hauling gravel with a wheelbarrow.

Then we went up to the cemetery to cut brush. We cleared it out and marked all the graves that I knew. Some of them we had to make up names for — the real old ones.

Last thing down here where this bridge is in town we planted a bunch of willows to hold the bank. Every spring run-off or heavy summer rain and that place would cave in more. Now those willows are tall and they saved the bank from caving. My mistake was planting too far down. I should have planted right against the cliff where there was nothing but mud. When I was a kid the bank used to be about 50 or 60 feet wide right above the flag pole. We used to play football there. Even adults played. Now the bank is so narrow that you can't even run a truck around there.

While we were working we used to have meetings once a week. I used to tell them about work. I'd say you have to have your mind on what you're doing at all times until you finish the job or you will get hurt. Carelessness is what hurts people. Makes accidents. As long as you're working at something that is real dangerous and you go think about something else you sure will get hurt. You can move any heavy object like house or warehouse or fish wheel, but you got to have your mind on it.

And the most important thing is never answer back your boss. If you answer back your boss, your boss get mad at you and pretty soon you don't know what you're doing. Your mind is not on the job you're doing. You're just thinking about that boss and what he's telling you. But that's what your boss is for. He's supposed to tell you what you're supposed to do. You're not supposed to answer him back. He know what he wants out of you, what you're supposed to do. That's why I'm hanging onto my job so long. There is times I get mad when my boss tell me what to do. I never answer him back. In my mind I always think I cannot do two jobs at one time. I finish one job. Then I go to the other job.

One time BIA asked me to be foreman on a job here. I don't want it. If I'm foreman I'll do more work than the guys that are working. I told them I'm going to help that electrician instead. They want a foreman but they couldn't get anybody. Finally they got a guy from Barrow. We asked him how he got the job and he said, "I've got two years of college. Maybe if I didn't have those two years of college, those guys wouldn't even talk to me."

That's what I explain to the young kids in the Youth Corps. When you start looking for any kind of a job, first thing they'll ask you is what grade you were in school. Just to see how smart you are. Probably you'd say you just went through high school. Maybe they wouldn't even talk to you. That's some experience I learned. Maybe they might give you something like pushing broom, like me, or shoveling snow. Shoveling some ditches or cut some brush. I could do that. I got no school, but I could do those things. But you kids are smarter than me. Maybe you went to eighth or seventh grade already and you have learned quite a bit. But still, at that, you ask for a job and they wouldn't even talk with you because you went only up to ninth grade in school. Just to high school.

And another thing, if you see that your boss is watching you dragging to work, or your boss tells you to do this and it takes you long time to figure out how to do it, you'll never made the grade. Just like in school, I tell them. And those kids sit down and listen to me as long as I'm talking. I try to help them think about their future.

Kaltag Front Street during break-up, 1982.

Kaltag February 1982.

1983 Kaltag Spring Carnival dog race at the opening chute.

At the dog race starting line. L-R: Adolph McGinty, Hazel, Don McCann, Marlene Madros.

Kaltag Front Street in springtime.

Approaching the finish line at the 1983 Kaltag Spring Carnival.

Earl Esmailka and Daniel Solomon racing in the Spring Carnival.

L-R: Simon Stanley, Junior Solomon, Sebastian McGinty Sr., Goodwin Semaken.

Index